Write Yourself Happy

Writing Short Fiction for Clarity, Creativity, and a Happier Life

Sally Dickson

Write Yourself Happy

Copyright © 2025 by Sally Dickson

The right of Sally Dickson to be identified as the Author of the Work has been asserted by her in accordance with the Copyright, Designs and Patents Act 1988.

A Dickson House Paperback

All rights reserved.

No part of this publication may be reproduced, distributed, or transmitted in any form or by any means, including photocopying, recording, or other electronic or mechanical methods, without the prior written permission of the publisher, nor be otherwise circulated in any form of binding or cover other than that in which it is published and without a similar condition being imposed on the subsequent purchaser. No part of this book may be reproduced or distributed in any form without prior written permission from the author, with the exception of non-commercial uses permitted by copyright law.

No part of this book may be reproduced or transmitted by any means, except as permitted by UK copyright law or the author. For licensing requests, please contact the author at www.flashfiction500.com.

The story, all names, characters, and incidents portrayed in this production are fictitious and any resemblance to real persons, living or dead, is purely coincidental.

Imprint: Mass Market Paperback
ISBN: 9798314171660

WRITE YOURSELF HAPPY

Typset in Atticus. Printed and bound in Great Britian by Ingram Spark part of Lightning Source UK Ltd

Lightning Source UK Ltd is committed to improving environmental performance by driving down CO2 emissions and reducing, reusing and recycling waste. Lightning Source UK Ltd recognizes that what we do today, affects the environment of both current and future generations and we are therefore committed to continuous environmental improvement. Our policy is to manage our businesses in such a manner as to have minimum impact on the environment in which we operate.

Book Cover and illustrations by Olu, of Bmcdesign on Fiverr.com

Contents

1. Why I wrote this book — 1
2. Welcome to Writing for Happiness — 3
3. Why Writing Makes You Happy — 7
4. Personal Stories of Transformation — 11
5. Writing as a Form of Therapy — 15
6. Finding Joy in Self-Expression — 17
7. The Courage to Begin — 19
8. The Writer's Mindset: Build Confidence, Stay Inspired — 23
9. The Basics of Writing — 27
10. Breathing for Writers: Clearing the Mind, Centring the Story — 31

11.	Finding Your Soundtrack: Writing to the Rhythm of You	35
12.	The Tools You Need to Write	41
13.	Recognising Your Unique Voice	47
14.	Setting Goals and Overcoming Blockers	51
15.	Writing Techniques to Express Yourself	55
16.	Feedback, Validation, and Defining Your Own Success	67
17.	Overcoming Writer's Block (Without Forcing It)	71
18.	Define What Will Make You Happy	75
19.	Technique in Short Storytelling	77
20.	Short Fiction: The Different Forms	79
21.	Why Short Fiction is So Appealing (and Joyful!)	81
22.	Short Fiction Isn't "Lesser" Than Novels—It's Different	83
23.	Writing Short Fiction for Happiness	85
24.	The Elements of a Great Short Story	87
25.	You Don't Need to Know Everything—Just Enough	93

26.	From Draft to Polish	95
27.	Technology Is Your Friend	103
28.	Tips and Tricks to Improve Your Happiness Through Writing	109
29.	Let Your Writing Be a Friend, Not a Test	111
30.	Growth Happens Quietly, Joyfully	113
31.	It's All a Story	115
32.	The Writer's Journey to Happiness	117
33.	Ten prompts to get you started	119
34.	Prompt 1. The Apricot Jam Years — Memoir	120
35.	Prompt 2. The Lieutenant's Letter — World War I	122
36.	Prompt 3. Ashes and Lace — Historical Romance	124
37.	Prompt 4. Lipstick on His Collar — Family Drama / Emotional Fiction	126
38.	Prompt 5. The Dragon Princess Drinks Tea Alone — Fantasy/Adventure	128
39.	Prompt 6. My Love, My Blade — Romantic Action/Adventure	130

40. Prompt 7. The Day I Left Him — Memoir/Emotional Realism — 132

41. Prompt 8. A Kitchen Like a Country — Domestic/Lyrical Fiction — 134

42. Prompt 9. Little Shoes, Big Goodbye — Parenting/Emotional Fiction — 136

43. Prompt 10. Wind in My Hair, Paris Behind Me — Reflective/Fictional Memoir — 138

Other Books by Same Author — 140

Chapter One
Why I wrote this book

I've been writing my whole life. Not always for anyone else—sometimes just for myself, late at night, in notebooks with pages falling out or on napkins in cafés when something suddenly needed to be said. Writing has always been the one thing that helps me make sense of the world, even when nothing else does. Simply put: writing keeps me sane.

It helps me breathe. It slows my racing thoughts. It brings me back to myself. Over time, I began to realise that writing—especially short fiction, those small, complete stories—offered not just creative satisfaction, but something deeper: a sense of calm. A kind of inner clarity. Even joy.

That's why I wrote this book.

I believe writing is for everyone, not just "writers." You don't need to publish or be perfect. You just need to show up with a few minutes, a pen, and a willingness to explore. Writing short fiction is a powerful, beautiful way to reconnect—with your imagination, your emotions, your voice.

I wanted to pass on the secret. To share what I've learned after years of scribbling, observing, starting again, and finding peace in the process. If even one person discovers joy or serenity through their own words because of this book, then it's done its job.

I hope it brings you light.

I wrote this book with a quiet hope—that you'll find peace in the pages.

> These words are a hand extended in the dark—a soft invitation to write your way back to joy.

Sally

Chapter Two
Welcome to Writing for Happiness

Hey there—welcome! You've just opened a book that believes writing isn't just something you *do*, it's something that can make you feel better, brighter, and more *you*. Whether you've got a story buzzing in your brain, a half-thought poem on the edge of your grocery list, or just a quiet urge to put pen to paper... you're in exactly the right place.

This isn't about chasing publishing deals or writing the next great novel (unless you want to—then yay, let's go!). It's about discovering how writing—especially short fiction—can be a surprisingly powerful path to **joy, calm, clarity**, and that feeling of "ahhh" when something inside finally gets said.

So why writing?

Because it works.

Writing helps us untangle thoughts, explore feelings, and understand ourselves just a little more deeply. It can reduce stress, clarify what matters, and offer a quiet, creative way to process the world. And beyond all that... it can be *fun*. Writing can feel playful. Satisfying. Even healing.

This book is your companion to building a writing life that lifts you up. You'll learn how to write regularly (without pressure), tap into your creativity, and discover what makes *your* stories uniquely yours. We'll cover simple tools, joyful techniques, and bite-sized ways to craft characters, explore plot, and shape satisfying little stories from just a few hundred to a few thousand words.

We're all about short fiction here—because it's manageable, flexible, and completely magic. You can start and finish something meaningful in a single sitting. And the best part? It doesn't have to be perfect. It just has to be *true to you*.

We'll also talk about finding your voice, setting small, happy writing goals, and connecting with others who love this stuff too. Because while writing often happens solo, the joy it brings? That's something we can absolutely share.

So if you're ready to feel a little lighter, a little more creative, and a whole lot more *you*—let's begin.

Just start. The joy comes with the first word.

As we begin this journey together, remember: Writing for Happiness isn't just about improving your writing—it's about improving your life. Whether you're jotting down story ideas in a notebook, finishing your first piece of fiction, or simply writing to see what shows up, you're stepping into something powerful, personal, and joyful.

Welcome to the adventure. Your stories are waiting.

> You don't need to write perfectly—you just need to begin. The joy comes with the first word.

Chapter Three
Why Writing Makes You Happy

Hey there fellow writer! So, you're thinking about writing—not just as a thing you do, but as something that actually makes you happier? I love that. Because the truth is, writing is *powerful*. More powerful than most people realize. It's not just about putting words on a page—it's about *feeling better*, *thinking clearer*, and sometimes even *figuring yourself out*.

Ever noticed how you feel lighter after journaling out your worries? Or how writing a silly poem or a heartfelt message to a friend lifts your mood? That's not just in your head—well, technically it *is*, but science backs it up! So, let's dive into why writing is like a secret happiness superpower just waiting for you to use it.

The Psychology of Writing and Happiness

Okay, let's get a little geeky for a second (but in a fun way, I promise). Scientists have actually studied the connection between writing and happiness, and what they've found is *wild*.

For starters, writing helps reduce stress. Studies show that when people write about their emotions—whether through journaling, storytelling, or even venting in an angry email they never send—it actually lowers their cortisol levels (that's the stress hormone that makes you feel like a frazzled mess).

And get this: writing doesn't just help in the moment—it has lasting effects. A famous study by psychologist James Pennebaker found that people who wrote about their thoughts and feelings for just 15-20 minutes a day reported feeling happier and even had **better physical health**. Yes, writing can literally boost your immune system.

Why? Because when you write, you process your emotions instead of letting them swirl around in your head like an endless loop of overthinking. It's like giving your brain a deep clean. And who doesn't love that fresh, organized feeling?

But it's not just about stress relief. Writing also triggers something called *the peak-end rule*. This means that when we look back on experiences, we remember the emotional *highs* and *endings* the most. So, when you write about good things—big or small—you reinforce those positive memories in your brain. It's like training your mind to focus on happiness.

Still with me? Good. Because now we're getting to the *really* fun part—real stories of how writing changes lives.

Chapter Four
Personal Stories of Transformation

Let's talk about real people whose lives have been totally turned around by writing. Because while the science is cool, it's the firsthand experiences that really hit home.

Meet Sarah: The Stressed-Out Overthinker

Sarah used to bottle up her stress like a shaken soda can. Work was overwhelming, and she found herself lying awake at night, her brain running in circles. Then one day, she decided to start journaling. Nothing fancy—just two paragraphs about her day, her thoughts, whatever was on her mind.

At first, she felt silly. But after a couple of weeks, she noticed something weird. She was *sleeping better*. Her mind felt *lighter*. That endless loop of worry? Slowing down.

Turns out, by writing things down, Sarah was actually *processing* her stress instead of just carrying it around like a heavy backpack. Fast forward a month, and she swears by her journal. It's her daily reset button—one she never knew she needed.

Jason: The Guy Who Found His Voice

Then there's Jason. Jason always felt like he had something to say, but he wasn't sure *how* to say it. He tried talking to friends, but words never came out quite right. Then, on a whim, he started drafting short stories. At first, they were just for him—little snippets of thoughts and feelings disguised as fiction.

Then one day, he shared a piece online. And people *connected* with it. They commented, shared their own experiences, told him how much his words meant to them. That was the moment Jason realized: writing wasn't just about getting things *out*—it was about *connecting* with others.

Now, writing is his outlet, his therapy, and his way of making sense of the world.

See? Writing doesn't just *help*—it *transforms*.

Chapter Five
Writing as a Form of Therapy

Now, I'm not saying writing replaces actual therapy (shoutout to the real therapists out there, you're amazing). But writing? It's definitely a free, always-available, judgment-free form of self-care.

Ever had a day where your emotions feel *huge* and *messy*, and you don't even know *why*? Writing helps untangle that mess. When you put feelings into words, they become more manageable—less like a tidal wave, more like a river you can navigate.

And you don't even have to write about yourself! Some people pour their emotions into poetry or stories. Others write letters they never send. There's no right or wrong way—just the simple magic of getting what's *inside* onto the *outside*.

Here's a little trick: Next time you're overwhelmed, grab a notebook (or open your Notes app) and do a five-minute brain dump. No filter, no structure—just pure, honest words. You'll be amazed at how much lighter you feel afterward.

Chapter Six

Finding Joy in Self-Expression

Here's the best part: Writing isn't just about working through tough stuff. It's also about *joy*.

Think about the last time you wrote something that made you smile—a funny text, a silly poem, a heartfelt note to a friend. Felt good, right? That's because creativity is *fun*.

When we write, we tap into something deeply human—the need to *express*. And that expression, whether it's through stories, jokes, or random doodles of words, is *pure joy*.

And guess what? You don't have to be a "great writer" to feel that joy. Writing is for *you*. It's your playground, your escape, your little corner of the world where anything is possible.

So, whether you're journaling, storytelling, or just jotting down nonsense that makes you laugh, keep at it. Because writing doesn't just make you *better*—it makes you *happier*.

And that, my friend, is reason enough to pick up that pen (or keyboard) and start writing.

Your Turn! I'd love to hear from you! Have you ever experienced the happiness-boosting effects of writing? Do you journal, write stories, or just scribble down thoughts for fun? Try it out and see what happens—you might just surprise yourself.

You don't have to write perfectly—just joyfully. Every silly sentence is a step toward feeling good.

Chapter Seven
The Courage to Begin

Overcoming Writer's Fear: From Blank Page to Brave Words

Okay, real talk: **writing fear is a thing**. And if you've ever stared at a blank page like it was a monster from a horror movie, you are *not* alone. Almost every writer—yes, even the famous ones with books on shelves—has felt that flutter of panic before starting.

But here's the thing: we're not authoring a 90,000-word novel or some masterpiece that's going to win literary awards (unless we want to one day, and then yay, go us!).

We're writing **short fiction**—just 300 to 3000 words. That's like, a single page to ten pages of a regular notebook. You could do it during a lunch break, curled up in bed, or in that weird in-between time when you're not quite ready to sleep but not quite ready to scroll TikTok either.

So, what's behind that fear? A few usual suspects:

- "What if it's bad?"

- "I don't know how to start."

- "I'm not really a writer."

- "What if people think it's cringe?"

Let's lovingly kick all those thoughts to the curb.

> The blank page isn't a monster—it's an invitation. You don't need perfect, just brave.

Tip #1. First Drafts are meant to be bad.

Seriously. First drafts are *meant* to be messy. They're the raw ingredients—not the cake. You don't judge a cake by how flour looks in the bowl, right? You stir it, bake it, and *then* it turns into something delicious. Same with writing.

Tip #2: Start anywhere.

If the beginning feels hard, skip it! Write a scene, a piece of dialogue, or even just a character sketch. You can always come back and shape it later. This is your playground—build your sandcastle however you want.

Tip #3: Make it small and light.

Remind yourself: "I'm just writing a short story. That's it." It doesn't have to change the world. It just has to be *yours*. Tell a silly story about a ghost in a library. Or a cozy scene of two people falling in love at a coffee shop. Let it be fun. Let it be light.

Tip #4: Treat fear like background noise.

You don't have to *fight* fear. Just acknowledge it: "Hey fear, I see you. Thanks for trying to protect me. But I'm gonna write anyway." Then keep typing.

The biggest secret? **You get braver the more you write**. Every tiny story is a little victory. You'll look back and realize: "Wow. I'm doing it." And you are.

Chapter Eight

The Writer's Mindset: Build Confidence, Stay Inspired

Let's talk mindset—the not-so-secret weapon behind every happy writer. Because writing isn't just about what you *do*, it's also about how you *think*.

Whether you're writing short fiction for fun, self-discovery, or someday sharing it with others, your mindset matters. So, here's the deal: you don't have to *be* confident to start. You just have to *show up*. Confidence comes *after* you write, not before. (Weird but true.)

So, what kind of mindset helps short fiction writers thrive?

Here are a few beliefs to adopt, like cozy sweaters for your brain:

1. "Done is better than perfect."

Perfection is the enemy of joy. The best short stories? They *exist*. They're not locked in someone's head, endlessly tweaked. They're finished, fun, and full of feeling. A story that's three hundred words and DONE will always be better than the 3000-word story you're too scared to start.

2. "My voice matters."

You don't have to sound like anyone else. You don't need fancy metaphors or ten-dollar words. What you bring to the page—your perspective, your humour, your heart—is already enough. Short fiction is all about *moments*. And nobody sees moments exactly like you do.

3. "Every story is practice."

Think of writing like going to the gym (but with snacks and pyjamas). Every session builds creative muscle. Don't worry about how "good" your story is—just keep showing up. You're getting stronger with every word.

4. "I can make this joyful."

Yes, writing can be deep and cathartic and all those serious things. But it can also be *play*. You're allowed to enjoy the process. Write the weird idea. Try the funny dialogue. Create a plot twist that makes *you* giggle. This is your space to explore.

> You are so allowed to take up creative space. To write for joy. To share or not share. To be messy, curious, and completely yourself.

And remember—we're not aiming for novels here. Just short fiction. One page. Ten pages max. That's it. No pressure. Just you, your imagination, and a few hundred words that didn't exist yesterday.

So go ahead—dare to write. You've got this.

Chapter Nine
The Basics of Writing

Making Time for Joyful Words (Even on Your Busiest Days)

Let's be honest—life is *busy*. Between work, laundry, catching up on texts, doomscrolling, and trying to remember to drink enough water, it can feel like there's just *no time* left for writing.

But here's the little secret most people don't realize **writing doesn't have to take hours**. You don't need a weekend writing retreat in the mountains or a three-hour uninterrupted block of silence (although, wow, dreamy). What do you need? A little consistency and a sprinkle of intention. That's it.

Remember: we're writing **short fiction** here. A single story might be three hundred words—that's barely more than a long Instagram caption. Or maybe it's three thousand words—that's ten pages in a notebook or a few solid writing sessions. Totally manageable. Totally worth it.

So, let's talk about how to fit this lovely little habit into your real, everyday life.

Tip 1: Tiny Time Blocks = Big Wins

You don't need to carve out a whole morning. You just need a **pocket of time**. Ten minutes with your coffee. Fifteen minutes before bed. Twenty minutes on a quiet Sunday afternoon.

Instead of thinking, *"I have no time to write,"* try flipping it:→ *"Where's a little moment I can claim today?"*

Even three 10-minute sessions a week adds up to 30 minutes of writing—and that's easily enough for a short story draft.

Tip 2: Pick a Day (or Two) That's "Writing Time".

Routine doesn't mean every day. It means *regularly*.

Choose one or two days a week that are your "writing days." Maybe Wednesday nights and Sunday mornings are your creative pockets. Mark them in your calendar like little joy dates with your imagination. Make it feel special—cozy drink, chill playlist, comfy hoodie.

You're not just squeezing writing in—you're *making space* for it.

Tip 3: Habit Stack It

This one's sneaky but powerful: pair writing with something you already do. Write for ten minutes *after your morning coffee.* Or *right before you scroll your phone at night.* Attach it to a habit that already lives in your day, and suddenly writing doesn't feel like a chore—it's just part of the rhythm.

Bonus: when your brain starts linking writing with that habit, it becomes automatic. Like brushing your teeth—but way more fun.

Tip 4: Make It Feel Light, Not Like Homework

This is creative playtime, not a high school essay. You're allowed to keep it low-pressure.

Write something silly. Start a story you don't plan to finish. Make it weird. Try a prompt just for fun. Write two hundred words and stop. That still counts.

The more joy you build into your writing habit, the more you'll *want* to come back to it. That's the key. Writing should feel like a gift to yourself—not another thing on your to-do list.

Tip 5: Track Progress in a Fun Way

Some people like calendars. Others love stickers, apps, or bullet journals. You don't need to be fancy—just find a way to *see* your progress.

Even just writing the date and "Wrote 300 words today!" in a notebook gives you that delicious sense of momentum. And momentum? That's magic.

Final Thought: Your Routine = Your Rhythm

You don't need to write every day. You don't need to write for hours. You *just* need to find your own little rhythm.

Short fiction is here for you whenever you show up. Three hundred words here, one thousand words there—it all adds up. And the more often you show up, the more your brain says, "Oh hey, we write now. Cool."

So, find your window. Light a candle, grab your pen, open that doc, and dive in. One short story at a time, you're building something beautiful.

You're not just making a routine—you're making a *home* for your creativity.

Chapter Ten

Breathing for Writers: Clearing the Mind, Centring the Story

Before the words come, we breathe.

Breathing is the simplest thing we do. We do it without thinking—thousands of times a day. But when we *do* think about it—when we slow it down, shape it with intention—it becomes one of the most powerful tools we have for calming the mind, clearing creative clutter, and finding focus.

For writers, especially, breath can act as a reset button. It brings you out of the noisy chatter in your head ("Am I good enough?" "Where is this story going?" "What if this is terrible?") and back into your body, your breath, the moment. Right where creativity happens.

You don't need candles or special music. Just a few quiet moments and your own lungs.

Here are a few breathing exercises you can try before you write—or anytime your mind feels messy, and your words feel far away.

1. The 4-7-8 Breath

A calming breath to quiet anxiety and invite focus.

This pattern activates your parasympathetic nervous system—your "rest and digest" mode.

- Breathe in through your nose for four seconds.

- Hold your breath for seven seconds.

- Exhale slowly through your mouth for eight seconds.

- Repeat 3–4 times.

Let your shoulders drop. Let your jaw unclench. You'll feel your thoughts slow down, like sediment settling in a glass of water.

2. Box Breathing (4-4-4-4)

A focused breath for balance and mental clarity.

This technique is used by everyone from yoga teachers to Navy SEALs—and yes, writers too.

- Inhale for 4 seconds
- Hold for four seconds.
- Exhale for 4 seconds
- Hold for four seconds.
- Repeat four times.

Picture a square if it helps—each side a part of the breath. It's steady, structured, and perfect for centring before a writing session.

3. Sighing Out the Static

A release breath to let go of mental noise.

This one's easy and surprisingly powerful:

- Inhale deeply through the nose.

- Exhale with a dramatic sigh through the mouth.

- Make it audible. Let it be a little ridiculous.

Do this 2–3 times. It physically and emotionally signals to your body: *we're letting go now*. Perfect before switching gears from daily stress to creative play.

Make It a Ritual

Before you write, take 2 minutes to breathe intentionally. Light a candle if you like. Stretch your neck. Breathe in silence. No phone. No pressure. Just breath and presence.

Let your first act of writing be breathing.

Because breath is story. It's rhythm. It's life. And when you breathe with intention, you create the space for your imagination to speak up—and for your words to follow.

> "Breathing is the best place to begin—slow down, clear the clutter, and make space for your words to arrive."

Chapter Eleven

Finding Your Soundtrack: Writing to the Rhythm of You

For writers, music can be a superpower, it's not just background noise—it's a creative tool. A vibe-setter. A mood-maker. A gentle block on the inner critic and a direct channel to your emotional core. For writers, music can act as an emotional shortcut. It lets you tap into joy, grief, longing, energy, and play *without* having to force anything.

There's something magical about finding the right song at the right moment. A chord strikes, a lyric lands, and suddenly—your fingers are flying across the page. The distractions fade. The doubts quiet down. The words come.

In short: the right soundtrack can unlock your story—and keep you coming back to the page.

- **Why Music Helps You Write**

First, it helps with **focus**. Pop on your headphones and suddenly, the world disappears. No noisy neighbours. No barking dog. No grocery list tapping you on the shoulder. Just you, the page, and the music.

Second, it helps with **emotion**. The right song can crack your heart open in a way a blank screen never could. It gives you access to feelings—and stories—you didn't even know were waiting.

And third, it sets the **tone** for your writing session. Want to write something fast-paced and sexy? Something sad and slow? Something whimsical and strange? Music is the secret portal to *that* exact energy.

- **Choose Your Mood, Choose Your Music**

Here are a few musical moods to explore—and what kinds of writing they pair beautifully with:

High-Energy, Bold & Sexy Writing

Turn to the icons: **Freddie Mercury**, **Meat Loaf**, **Lizzo**, **Lady Gaga**. These artists bring drama, tempo, and a fearless edge. Perfect for writing steamy scenes, bold characters, or action with flair.

Try: *Don't Stop Me Now, I'd Do Anything for Love, Juice*

Romantic & Reflective Themes

If you're writing love letters, soft scenes, or bittersweet longing, lean into **Adele**, **Simon & Garfunkel**, or even a little **Norah Jones**. These tunes invite a slower pace and deeper emotional resonance.

Try: *Make You Feel My Love, The Sound of Silence, Come Away With Me*

Feel-Good, Warm, & Uplifting

For upbeat, hopeful stories—or just to remind yourself why you love writing—turn to **Taylor Swift**, **Ed Sheeran**, or **Ben Rector**. These are songs that hug your heart and make writing feel light.

Try: *Daylight, Castle on the Hill, Brand New*

Ambient, Epic, & Cinematic Writing

If you want to disappear into another world—fantasy, historical, gothic—turn to ambient film scores and medleys from your favourite fandoms: **LOTR**, **Game** of Thrones**, **Disney**, **Bridgerton**, **Studio Ghibli**. No lyrics, just vibes.

Try: Howard Shore's *Rohan Theme*, Bridgerton's classical pop covers, or the *Interstellar* soundtrack

- **Make a Playlist Just for You**

Create themed playlists for different writing moods or projects:

- "Epic Fantasy Battle"

- "Soft Sad Romance"

- "Heroine With a Sword"

- "Cozy Café Journaling"

When you return to a playlist, your brain remembers: *this is writing time.* It becomes a gentle ritual—a cue that it's time to create.

Final Note: Let the Music Inspire You

Don't just use music as a tool—let it surprise you. Let it *lead*. Start a story based on a lyric. Write a character inspired by a song. Or just hit shuffle and let the emotion guide your fingers.

Whatever your writing mood, your soundtrack is out there, waiting to be played.

So, plug in, press play, and write the scene you didn't know you had in you.

> "Music is your creative co-pilot—choose the soundtrack that lifts your mood, fuels your story, and quiets your doubt."

Chapter Twelve
The Tools You Need to Write

Hint: You probably already have them.

People often think writers need perfect setups: a mahogany desk, antique typewriter, vintage mug filled with artisan coffee, and at least three candles lit for atmosphere.

But honestly? The best tools for writing are often scrappy, spontaneous, and already in your pocket—or under your coffee cup.

The truth is: **writing doesn't wait for ideal conditions.** It sneaks up on you in the middle of your commute, while you're folding laundry, or in the quiet, thoughtful moment after your friend says something that hits you like a poem. That's why the best writers aren't the ones with the fanciest software. They're the ones ready to *catch the moment.*

Let's talk about the simple, powerful tools that help you do exactly that.

1. Napkins, Menus, and Till Receipts

Yes, seriously.

The best stories start as scribbled fragments—half-lines, overheard dialogue, a sudden memory—captured on whatever's closest. A napkin. A receipt. The blank side of a menu you weren't supposed to write on.

These are not "lesser" tools. They are proof that you were *present*. You were listening. And you wrote it down before the idea fluttered away. Writers are collectors of moments, and sometimes the quickest net is a crumpled scrap in your pocket.

So, write on the margins. Capture that spark. Transcribe it later, sure—but *honour* the scribble.

2. The Notebook and Pen: Non-Negotiable

Every writer should have a notebook. Not necessarily a fancy one (though if that sparks joy, go for it). Just one that you love enough to use.

Notebooks are where you collect the *raw stuff*—your ideas, images, snippets of scenes, titles that sound delicious but don't yet belong to anything. A pen in your hand gives you a kind of freedom that typing can't. It's quiet. It's personal. It slows you down enough to notice what you're really thinking.

Keep your notebook close. Let it become your creative sidekick. It doesn't have to be tidy—it just has to be *yours*.

3. The Record Button on Your Phone

Ideas don't always arrive when your hands are free. That's where your phone's voice recorder comes in.

Dictate a line while you're walking the dog. Capture that character's perfect one-liner before the red light turns green. Ramble about your story idea while you're making toast.

Your recorded voice doesn't have to be polished—it just has to *exist*. Use voice memos like idea jars. Later, you can revisit them and pull-out gold you forgot you had.

(Plus, there's something oddly charming about hearing your past self-whisper a plot twist at 7 a.m. while half-asleep.)

4. The Computer: Your Writing Studio in a Box

Once the idea is captured, the real shaping begins—and that's where your computer shines.

Yes, you can type. But you can also:

- **Dictate** entire paragraphs using built-in voice-to-text tools.

- **Transcribe** voice notes into story starts.

- **Edit and revise** with ease—cutting, copying, rearranging without fear.

- **Use tools** like Read Aloud to hear your work aloud.

- **Back up** your work so it never gets lost in a coffee-stained notebook.

And of course, your computer connects you to the world: writing groups, publishing platforms, contests, prompts, playlists. It's a full creative hub.

Final Thought: Use What You Have

Writing tools are just that—*tools*. The magic lives in *you*. Whether you're jotting notes on a napkin, whispering into your phone, or editing chapter seven at midnight, the most important thing is that you're writing.

So be resourceful. Be a little messy. Capture the spark, however it comes.

And remember: *the story doesn't care what you write it on—it just wants to be told.*

> "Don't wait for perfect tools. Use what you have, scribble what you can, and trust the story will follow."

Chapter Thirteen
Recognising Your Unique Voice

Finding your writing voice is a little like finding your favourite pair of shoes—not necessarily the flashiest or the fanciest, but the ones that *fit*. When you slip into your voice, you'll know. Not because someone told you it's good, but because something inside you *settles*.

There's a sense of calm. A quiet confidence. A feeling that says, *"Yes. This is mine."*

Your voice is not about perfect grammar or clever phrases—it's about rhythm, emotion, and honesty. It's the way you observe the world. The images you return to. The cadence of your thoughts on the page.

One of the surest signs you've tapped into your voice is the **flow**. The words come quicker, cleaner, like they've been waiting just below the surface. Time blurs. You stop second-guessing. You're not trying to sound like anyone else. You're just writing—and it feels *right*.

And then comes the emotion.

Sometimes it's a lump in your throat. Sometimes it's a quiet joy, or even laughter at your own wit. It swells up unexpectedly, reminding you that this—*this*—is why you write.

That moment is gold.

Your voice will evolve over time. It will shift with your moods, your seasons, your life. But when you find that feeling—that stillness, that flow, that spark—you've found something uniquely yours.

> Hold onto it. Write from there. That's where the magic lives.

Your voice is like your laugh—uniquely yours, slightly odd, and completely perfect when you stop trying to control it.

You will feel like a deep exhale—steady, clear, and full of something that matters.

Chapter Fourteen
Setting Goals and Overcoming Blockers

Writing Without Pressure, Creating Without Panic.

Okay, let's get cozy and talk about two things that can either *help* your writing or totally *derail* it: **goals** and **blocks**.

On one hand, goals are amazing. They give you structure, motivation, and that satisfying "look what I did!" feeling. But on the other hand, if they're too big or vague? They can turn into little guilt monsters that make you want to run away from your notebook entirely.

And then there's writer's block—the dreaded blank stare at the screen, the "everything I write is trash" voice, the sudden urge to deep-clean your entire kitchen instead of writing *one* sentence. Yeah. We've all been there.

But here's the good news: with the right mindset and structure, you can *absolutely* set writing goals that feel fun, flexible, and totally doable—and you can outsmart those blocks when they pop up. Promise.

Setting Writing Goals That *Actually Work*

Let's start with the goals. Forget about perfection. Forget about daily word counts that would scare even a full-time author. We're writing *short fiction*, remember? Just three hundred–three thousand words. That's a story you can finish in a day or stretch out over comfy writing sessions.

Here's how to make your writing goals feel like gentle guideposts, not scary deadlines:

1. Make It Tiny and Clear

Bad goal: "I should write more." Good goal: "I'll write one 500-word story by next Sunday."

Even better? Tie it to a prompt or theme: → "I'll write a 1000-word story about a secret meeting in a bookstore."

Now it's specific, fun, and bite-sized. Like a little creative snack.

2. Think in Story Chunks

Instead of measuring your success by days or word counts, try thinking in *stories*.

→ "This month, I'll write two short stories." → "This week, I'll start and finish one micro fiction piece."

Every time you finish a story—no matter the length—you get a little dopamine hit, a tiny win. And that momentum adds up *fast*.

3. Create a "Goal Buffet".

Not in the mood to write one thousand words today? No problem. Give yourself options.

Your "writing goal buffet" might include:

- Write two hundred words.

- Edit a previous piece.

- Try a new prompt.

- Write a character monologue.

- Make a list of story ideas.

You're still moving forward, even if you're doing it sideways. And that counts!

Chapter Fifteen

Writing Techniques to Express Yourself

Finding Your Voice Through Stories, Poems, Posts, and Play

Okay, so by now, you've probably realized something kind of wonderful: **writing isn't just one thing**. It's not just short stories or novels or essays. It's *everything* from a single sentence that makes someone laugh to a poem that cracks your heart wide open.

The beautiful thing about writing is that there are *so many* ways to express yourself. Different moods, different messages,different days—each one can be matched with a writing style that helps you saywhat you really want to say.

Whether you're working through emotions, telling astory that's been in your head for years, or just goofing around with sillyrhymes—there's a writing form for *you*.

And guess what? You're allowed to try them all.

You Don't Have to Stick to One Style

Just like you wear different clothes for different moods, you can use different writing styles for different feelings or ideas.Here's a little sampler platter of the ways you can express yourself throughwords—no pressure to pick just one.

Short Fiction (300–3000words)

You already know this one—we've been talking about itall along! A tiny, self-contained story with a beginning, middle, and end. Itcan be dramatic, funny, weird, magical, romantic—*whatever you want.*Think of it as a slice of cake instead of the whole bakery. Perfectlysatisfying, and totally doable.

Monologues & Dialogues

Want to get inside a character's head? Try writing a *monologue*—a short, emotional speech from one person's point of view. Great for exploring thoughts, feelings, or confessions.

Or, want to make it more dynamic? Write a *dialogue*—just two characters talking. No need for narration, just their voices on the page. You'll be amazed at what shows up.

Children's Stories

Simple language, big imagination, deep heart. Writing for children is magical. You can tell a whimsical story, sneak in a life lesson, or create a whole new world in just a hundred words. Bonus: it helps you reconnect with your own inner child.

Playlets & Screenplays

Feeling theatrical? Try a *playlet*—a short scene meant for the stage—or a mini *screenplay*. Focus on action, dialogue, and stage directions. It's a fun way to "see" your story like a little movie in your mind.

Poetry, Haikus, andLimericks

Poetry is *pure emotion in concentrated form*.

- A **haiku** (5-7-5 syllables) can capture a moment or feeling in just seventeen syllables.

- A **limerick** is great for humour and rhythm—think five-line rhymes that bounce.

- And free-form **poetry**? That's your soul on the page. There are *no rules*, just rhythm, image, and truth.

- Whether it's serious or silly, poetry is a powerful-way to say what can't be said any other way.

Blogs & Journals

Have something to say about your day, your thoughts,or your life? Blog it. Or journal it. Whether it's private or shared,reflective or rant, this kind of writing helps you *connect*—to yourselfor to others.

It doesn't have to be formal or polished. It just hasto be *real*.

Instagram Posts, Facebook Stories & Social Writing

Yes, this counts as writing! If you've ever poured your heart into an Instagram caption, shared a story on Facebook that made people laugh or cry, or crafted a little nugget of truth for your feed—you're already a storyteller.

Micro-stories, emotional reflections, even a funny post about your cat—they're all ways of expressing your unique voice.

How to Choose the Right Form?

Ask yourself:

→ What do I want to say?

→ How do I want to *feel* while saying it?

→ Who am I writing it for—just me, or someone else?

You might want to write a poem about grief one day, and a comedic dialogue the next. That's the beauty of it—writing gives you *options*. No form is better than another. They're simply different tools in your creative toolbox.

Final Thought: You Get to Play

This part is all about *freedom*. You get to *try things*. Explore. Experiment. Mix forms, break rules, start over. There's no "right" way to express yourself through writing—only the ways that feel *right for you*.

So go write that monologue. Post that poem. Start a blog. Tell a story from a child's point of view. Write a 5-line limerick about your cat being a drama queen. Write your truth. Or write pure nonsense for the joy of it.

> Because this isn't about being perfect.
> It's about being *you*

Finding Your Voice Through Stories, Poems, Posts, and Play

Okay, so by now, you've probably realized something kind of wonderful: **writing isn't just one thing**. It's not just short stories or novels or essays. It's *everything* from a single sentence that makes someone laugh to a poem that cracks your heart wide open.

The beautiful thing about writing is that there are *so many* ways to express yourself. Different moods, different messages,different days—each one can be matched with a writing style that helps you saywhat you really want to say.

Whether you're working through emotions, telling astory that's been in your head for years, or just goofing around with sillyrhymes—there's a writing form for *you*.

And guess what? You're allowed to try them all.

You Don't Have to Stick to One Style

Just like you wear different clothes for different moods, you can use different writing styles for different feelings or ideas.Here's a little sampler platter of the ways you can express yourself throughwords—no pressure to pick just one.

Short Fiction (300–3000words)

You already know this one—we've been talking about itall along! A tiny, self-contained story with a beginning, middle, and end. Itcan be dramatic, funny, weird, magical, romantic—*whatever you want.*Think of it as a slice of cake instead of the whole bakery. Perfectlysatisfying, and totally doable.

Monologues & Dialogues

Want to get inside a character's head? Try writing a *monologue*—ashort, emotional speech from one person's point of view. Great for exploringthoughts, feelings, or confessions.
Or, want to make it more dynamic? Write a *dialogue*—just two characterstalking. No need for narration, just their voices on the page. You'll be amazed at what shows up.

Children's Stories

Simple language, big imagination, deep heart. Writingfor children is magical. You can tell a whimsical story, sneak in a lifelesson, or create a whole new world in just a hundred words. Bonus: it helpsyou reconnect with your own inner child.

Playlets & Screenplays

Feeling theatrical? Try a *playlet*—a short scenemeant for the stage—or a mini *screenplay*. Focus on action, dialogue, andstage directions. It's a fun way to "see" your story like a little movie inyour mind.

Poetry, Haikus, andLimericks

Poetry is *pure emotion in concentrated form*.

- A **haiku** (5-7-5 syllables) can capture a moment or feeling in just seventeen syllables.

- A **limerick** is great for humour and rhythm—think five-line rhymes that bounce.

- And free-form **poetry**? That's your soul on the page. There are *no rules*, just rhythm, image, and truth.

- Whether it's serious or silly, poetry is a powerfulway to say what can't be said any other way.

Blogs & Journals

Have something to say about your day, your thoughts,or your life? Blog it. Or journal it. Whether it's private or shared,reflective or rant, this kind of writing helps you *connect*—to yourselfor to others.

It doesn't have to be formal or polished. It just hasto be *real*.

Instagram Posts,Facebook Stories & Social Writing

Yes, this counts as writing! If you've ever pouredyour heart into an Instagram caption, shared a story on Facebook that madepeople laugh or cry, or crafted a little nugget of truth for your feed—you'realready a storyteller.

Micro-stories, emotional reflections, even a funnypost about your cat—they're all ways of expressingyour unique voice.

How to Choose the RightForm?

Ask yourself:
→ What do I want to say?
→ How do I want to *feel* while saying it?
→ Who am I writing it for—just me, or someone else?

You might want to write a poem about grief one day, and a comedic dialogue the next. That's the beauty of it—writing gives you *options*. No form is better than another. They're simply different tools in your creative toolbox.

Final Thought: You Get to Play

This part is all about *freedom*. You get to *try things*. Explore. Experiment. Mix forms, break rules, start over. There's no "right" way to express yourself through writing—only the ways that feel *right for you*.

So go write that monologue. Post that poem. Start a blog. Tell a story from a child's point of view. Write a 5-line limerick about your cat being a drama queen. Write your truth. Or write pure nonsense for the joy of it.

> Because this isn't about being perfect.
> It's about being *you*

Chapter Sixteen

Feedback, Validation, and Defining Your Own Success

Because You Don't Need a Standing Ovation to Feel Proud of What You Wrote

Let's have a real moment: you've written something. You finished it. Maybe it's three hundred words, maybe it's three thousand. That is *huge*. That is *enough*. And now you might be wondering:

"Should I show this to someone?"

"Is it even any good?"

"What if no one cares?"

Totally normal thoughts. We all want to feel seen. We want someone to read our words and go, "Wow, this is *amazing*!" (Cue applause, dramatic spotlight, maybe a book deal?)

But here's the truth: **you don't need a thunderous reaction to feel proud of your writing**. And honestly, most writers—even published ones—don't get that kind of response every time.

So, what do we do instead? We shift our focus to what really matters: *your own happiness and growth*. Let's talk about how to approach feedback and validation in a way that supports your creativity instead of squashing it.

Start With the *Only* Goal That Matters First: Finish It

Before you even *think* about feedback, the very first goal should be: **finish the piece**.

Not "make it perfect." Not "wow the world." Just *finish it*.

Because finishing something you started? That's the win. That's the satisfaction. That's you showing up for yourself. Every time you do that; you build confidence and trust in your creativity. That's gold.

Then Ask Yourself: *What Do I Want Next?*

Once your story is done (woohoo!), you've got options. This is the "choose your own adventure" part. Each one has a different flavour of feedback, depending on what you're craving. Here are the paths:

Publish It (Just for Fun)

Post it on a personal blog, a family blog, a shared Google Doc, or a social media page. Let it live in the world. You don't need a huge following. You don't need fancy formatting.→ The goal: *expression*, not approval.Just the act of sharing your voice can be a joyful experience.

Share It With People You Trust

If you want *supportive eyes*, send it to a friend, family member, or writing buddy. Let them know what kind of feedback you're looking for. (Like: "Please just tell me what you liked" or "Let me know if it made sense.") You're allowed to set boundaries.

Submit It to a Competition

There are tons of short story competitions, and some even offer optional critiques for $10–20. That's a pretty cool way to get thoughtful feedback from people who read your writing—and it gives you a sense of structure and purpose too.

Pro tip: Even if you don't win or place, you *finished* something and put it out into the world. That's more than most people ever do.

Keep It Private—That's Valid Too

Not every piece needs to be shared. Writing is just for you. A gift to your future self. A time capsule of who you are right now. And that's more than enough.

Chapter Seventeen

Overcoming Writer's Block (Without Forcing It)

Let's talk about the Big Baddie: **Writer's Block**. First of all—if you've hit it, it doesn't mean you're not a "real" writer. It means you're a *human* writer.

But here's the thing, writer's block isn't about a lack of ideas. It's about *pressure*. Pressure to be good. To get it "right." To create something impressive. And that pressure? It shuts down creativity faster than a Wi-Fi outage in the middle of a deadline.

So, let's loosen it up.

Here Are Go-To Tools to Get Unstuck:

1. Write the Worst Version Possible

Seriously. Sit down and *intentionally* write the most ridiculous, awkward, cringe-worthy version of your story. It's hilarious. It's freeing. And weirdly, it often leads to something *really good*.

2. Use a Prompt or Constraint

Sometimes we get blocked because the page is *too open*. Give yourself a little fence and suddenly your creativity starts bouncing off the walls in fun ways.

→ "Write a 300-word story with only dialogue."

→ "Write a story where the main character is stuck in a waiting room."

→ "Start with the line: 'I didn't mean to steal it.'"

3. Change Formats

Try switching mediums:

→ Write by hand for a change

→ Type in a different font

→ Use voice-to-text and ramble your story out loud

Sometimes just shaking up the method opens new doors in your brain.

4. Take a Break—On Purpose

Go for a walk, take a shower, do something *not* writing. Blocks often clear when your brain's off duty. But set a time to return. (Like, "Okay, back to it at 4:30 with a cup of tea.")

Final Pep Talk: Your Pace, Your Process

Writing goals should motivate, not intimidate. And blocks? They're just speed bumps, not stop signs.

Set small, clear goals that fit into your life. Give yourself permission to write badly, write short, write weird. That's how magic happens.

You don't need to write daily. You don't need to be brilliant every time. You just need to keep showing up—one page, one story, one moment of creativity at a time.

And hey, you're already doing it.

Chapter Eighteen
Define What Will Make You Happy

Here's the biggest, most important truth: **You get to decide what success looks like.**

- Maybe it's just finishing the story.

- Maybe it's hitting "publish" on your blog.

- Maybe it's writing something you're proud of, even if no one else reads it.

Ask yourself:→ *"What would make me feel good about this?"*→ *"What do I want to get out of writing today?"*

When you define your own version of success, you stop needing other people to validate it. And ironically? That's when the joy really starts to grow.

One Final Reminder: Your Joy Is Not Up for Debate

You're allowed to write badly. You're allowed to write weirdly. You're allowed to write something no one else understands or likes—*and still be proud of it.*

Feedback is a tool, not a verdict. Applause is lovely, but it's not the goal. Happiness, growth, expression, *fun*—those are the goals.

So go ahead: finish the story. Post it. Don't post it. Enter a contest. Print it out and tape it to your fridge. Dance around the room because you did something brave and creative.

You wrote. You made something from nothing. And that's amazing.

Chapter Nineteen
Technique in Short Storytelling

What is Short Fiction?

Defining Short Fiction and Its Unique Appeal

So, let's start with the basics. What exactly *is* short fiction?

Short fiction is storytelling in its most compact, potent form. Think of it like an espresso shot of creativity—small, but powerful. Unlike novels, which sprawl across chapters and subplots and pages and pages of backstory, short fiction delivers a full narrative experience—beginning, middle, and end—in a **tight word count**, usually between

300 and 3000 words. It's a complete story you can write in a day and read in five minutes.

And the best part? **It's accessible to everyone.** You don't need months of free time or a whole plot outline to get started. You just need an idea, a spark, and a little window of time.

Chapter Twenty
Short Fiction: The Different Forms

Short fiction wears many hats. It includes a range of forms and styles, all of them with their own vibe and rhythm. Here are ways it shows up:

- **Micro fiction**: Super short—sometimes as little as one hundred words. These pieces often focus on a single moment or emotion. Perfect for squeezing into your day.

- **Flash Fiction**: Usually under one thousand words. Flash is snappy, vivid, and often packs a surprising twist or emotional punch.

- **Traditional Short Stories**: 1000 to 3000 words (or a little more if you're feeling fancy). These give you room to develop characters and plot, while still being tight and efficient.

- **Vignettes or Scenes**: These might not follow a full narrative arc but instead give a snapshot of a mood, setting, or character.

And don't forget—short fiction can also be playful with format: → Written as a letter → Told through text messages → Structured like a script or diary entry → Or even a poem-disguised-as-a-story.

Short fiction is about *freedom*. You can experiment, explore, and say exactly what you want without the pressure of 80,000 words and a publishing deal.

Chapter Twenty-One

Why Short Fiction is So Appealing (and Joyful!)

Short fiction is *deeply satisfying*, both to write and to read. Here's why:

1. It's Quick to Create and Quick to Share

This is writing you can *actually finish*—even in a busy life. You don't need to commit to a whole novel. Just carve out a couple of hours, and boom, you've got a finished piece.

2. It's Intimate and Focused

Short stories tend to zoom in on one moment, one theme, one emotional truth. That kind of focus creates a sense of intensity, even in a gentle story. Readers often *feel* short stories more deeply because there's no filler—just heart.

3. It's an Amazing Way to Improve Your Writing

Writing short fiction sharpens your skills *fast*. You have to learn to be clear, concise, and emotionally resonant with fewer words. It's like strength training for writers. Every story is a mini masterclass.

4. It's Accessible to Readers Too

In today's busy world, a short story is something people actually have time to read. Share it in an email, post it on your blog, read it aloud to a friend. You get immediate connection and feedback—which is so motivating.

Chapter Twenty-Two

Short Fiction Isn't "Lesser" Than Novels—It's Different

Some people think short fiction is just a stepping stone to longer works. Nope. It's a powerful, professional, artful form in its own right. Think of the literary greats—Raymond Carver, Alice Munro, Shirley Jackson, Lydia Davis—*experts in* the short form.

Short fiction lets you explore all kinds of themes without the weight of a full novel. You can tell *bold* stories. You can try *weird* formats. You can write something just for you and feel completely fulfilled.

And if you *do* dream of writing longer works someday? Guess what—short fiction is the *perfect* way to practice. You learn to build worlds, shape characters, and create tension—all in a tidy little container.

Who Is Short Fiction *For*?

The answer is: **everyone.**

- Beginners who want to start writing but feel overwhelmed by the idea of a novel.

- Busy people who only have small pockets of time to create

- Writers who want to explore different genres, moods, and ideas

- Storytellers who want to share moments, messages, or memories

- Artists who want to feel *joy* in the act of creating

Whether you're writing to heal, to play, to connect, or to grow—short fiction welcomes you with open arms.

Chapter Twenty-Three

Writing Short Fiction for Happiness

Writing Short Fiction for Happiness

At the heart of it, *short fiction is joyfully manageable*. And when you write short pieces regularly, you start to develop a rhythm. You feel the thrill of finishing. You start looking at the world differently—spotting stories in overheard conversations, strange dreams, tiny observations.

It makes you feel *awake*.

And when the goal is writing to feel happier, to feel more like *yourself*? Short fiction is the perfect companion. Low pressure. High impact. Full of possibility.

CHAPTER TWENTY-FOUR

The Elements of a Great Short Story

H*ow to Craft Compelling Characters, Plots, and Settings in a Small Space*

So, you've decided to write a short story (yay!), and now you're wondering: *how do I actually make it good?* Or at least *coherent?* Maybe even *kind of amazing?*

Here's the thing about short fiction: it may be short, but that doesn't mean it's simple. In fact, drafting a satisfying story in just 300 to 3000 words is a little like cooking a delicious meal with only few ingredients—you've got to choose each one with care and make every sentence *count*.

But don't worry—this isn't about writing perfectly. This is about writing *effectively*. With just few tools and a little bit of craft know-how, you can shape your story into something that *feels* complete, satisfying, and—most importantly—true to *you*.

Let's break down the key ingredients that make a short story great.

1. Character: The Beating Heart of Your Story

Every exceptional story starts with someone we care about. That doesn't mean they have to be likable or perfect—it just means they have to be *real*.

In short fiction, you don't have space to describe a character's whole life history. So instead, focus on *essence*. Give us just enough to understand:

- What they want

- What they fear

- What's standing in their way.

You can reveal character through:

- A choice they make.

- A line of dialogue

- A vivid detail (they wear glitter socks to funerals = we immediately know something about them!)

Start small but make it specific. Characters don't need long bios—they need *energy* and *emotion*.

Ask yourself: → What does this character want *right now*? → What's the one thing they *wouldn't* say out loud—but feel deeply?

2. Plot: A Problem, a Shift, a Resolution

Plot doesn't have to be complicated, especially in short fiction. In fact, keeping it simple often makes it more powerful. All you need is this classic formula:

A character wants something → Something gets in the way → Something changes.

That's it. That's your story arc.

You can make it as dramatic or quiet as you like:

- A girl loses her voice before an audition (external conflict)

- A man realizes he's in love with his best friend (internal shift)

- A child finds a stray dog and has to decide whether to keep it (moral dilemma)

The key is to **start with tension**—something unsolved, unfinished, or unspoken—and let the story move toward *change*.

Change can be big, or it can be tiny but meaningful. The main thing is by the end, something's different. The character, the world, the reader.

Ask yourself:→ What's at stake here—even if it's just emotional?→ What moment is this story *really* about?

3. Setting: Make It Vivid in Bold Strokes

You don't need paragraphs of description to create atmosphere. One or two well-chosen details can *set the entire scene*. Think of setting as the emotional backdrop to your story.

Is it moody and rainy? Bright and buzzing? Still and tense?

Use **sensory details** to pull us in:

- The squeak of a bike tire on wet pavement

- The tang of salt in the air at the harbour

- The scratchy warmth of a grandma's wool blanket

Don't overload the reader—just *anchor* the story in a place we can picture.

Ask yourself: → What does this world *feel* like? → What's one detail that tells me everything I need to know?

4. Dialogue: Keep It Snappy and Real

In a short story, dialogue does heavy lifting. It reveals character, moves the plot forward, and keeps the pace lively.

Here's the golden rule: **only write what someone would actually say**—and keep it tight.

Realistic doesn't mean boring. It means *authentic*. People rarely say exactly what they mean. Use that.

Example:Instead of: "I'm afraid I'm in love with you." Try: "Do you ever think about... what it would be like, if it was just us?"

Use dialogue to hint, not spell everything out. That space between the lines? That's where emotion lives.

Ask yourself: → What's unsaid in this conversation? → How can I make their voice feel *alive*?

5. Theme: What's the Story *Really* About?

You don't need to hit readers over the head with your "message," but it helps to know: *why am I telling this story?*

Maybe it's about:

- Longing

- Forgiveness

- Letting go.

- Connection

- Hope

Whatever it is, keep it in the back of your mind as you write. When every element—character, plot, setting, dialogue—is in service of that emotional truth, the story will resonate more deeply.

6. Pacing: Every Word Earns Its Place

Short fiction is lean by design. That means every sentence should serve a purpose—whether it's moving the plot forward, deepening character, or building mood. If a sentence isn't doing *something*, it might not need to be there.

But don't mistake "tight" for "dry." You can still be playful, poetic, or lush—just make sure it's *intentional*.

Tip: Read your story out loud. You'll instantly hear where it drags or where the rhythm sings.

Chapter Twenty-Five
You Don't Need to Know Everything—Just Enough

Short stories are slices of life. We don't need to know your character's backstory from birth. We just need a glimpse of them in a moment that matters.

Start in the middle. Trust your reader to fill in the blanks. Trust *yourself* to know what this story wants to be.

And remember great short stories aren't about size. They're about *impact*. One moment. One shift. One image that sticks with the reader.

That's all it takes to make something uniquely beautiful.

Chapter Twenty-Six

From Draft to Polish

How to Revise and Refine Short Fiction for Clarity, Impact, and Joy

Okay, so you did the hard part—you actually wrote the thing. That rough, messy, imperfect draft? That's a *win*. You created something from nothing. That's a big deal.

But now you're staring at it thinking, "What happens next? Is it any good? Do I need to fix it? How do I *fix* it?"

First of all, deep breath. Revising isn't about tearing your work apart—it's about shaping it so the story inside shines a little brighter. It's like cleaning the dust off a beautiful little gem you just dug up. The sparkle is already there—you're just helping it show.

And in the world of short fiction—300 to 3000 words—revising doesn't have to feel overwhelming. You're working with a small, manageable piece of writing. You can read it in one sitting. You can revise it in layers. You can make real improvements *without* losing your mind (or your joy).

Let's talk about how to polish your short story in a way that's gentle, doable, and even... fun.

Step 1: Celebrate the Draft

Before you change *anything*, pause to appreciate what you just did. You finished a story. That alone is worth a little dance, a high five, or a victory tea.

Too many writers rush into editing with a "what's wrong with it?" mindset. Try this instead:→ *What's working? What do I love about this? Where does the story feel alive?*

Start with self-kindness. It sets the tone for everything that comes next.

Step 2: Read It Like a Reader

Let your story sit for a day or two (if you can). Then come back and read it with fresh eyes—*not as the writer*, but as a curious reader.

Ask yourself:

- What's happening in this story?

- Did anything confuse me?

- When did I *feel* something?

- Is there a clear beginning, middle, and end?

- Is the main character clear? Are their wants and obstacles clear?

- Do I *care* about what happens?

Don't get bogged down in grammar or typos yet. This first read is all about clarity and connection.

Pro tip: reading it *out loud* is pure magic. You'll hear where the flow stumbles, where the emotion lands, and where the story sings.

Step 3: Big Picture Fixes First

Once you've read through, focus on the big stuff:

- **Structure:** Does it have a strong shape? (Beginning → Something Happens → Change or Realization)

- **Character clarity:** Do we know what your main character wants and feels?

- **Emotion and tension:** Is there *movement*—not necessarily action, but change?

- **Theme:** Is there a consistent emotional thread or message?

Ask yourself: → Is this the story I *meant* to tell?

If the answer is "sort of," great! Now shape it to get closer to your original spark.If the answer is "not really," that's okay too—you might have discovered a different story along the way.

Step 4: Trim the Fat (But Keep the Flavour)

In short fiction, **every word matters**. So, now's the time to tighten things up.

Go through your draft looking for:

- Repetition (did you say the same thing twice?)

- Over-explaining (can the reader infer it without being told?)

- Weak or filler words (like "very," "really," "just," "a little," and more...)

- Dialogue that doesn't move the story forward.

That said—don't cut out the flavour! If a sentence *sparkles* or makes you smile, keep it. The goal isn't to make your story bland—it's to make it clean and clear.

Step 5: Line-Level Magic

Now that the bones of the story are strong, it's time to polish the *language*. This is where you can play with rhythm, tone, and imagery. It's the difference between "fine" and "oooh, that's lovely."

Tips for line-level editing:

- Swap out vague verbs for vivid ones.

- Replace clichés with original images.

- Read sentences aloud for flow—tighten where needed.

- Play with punctuation and formatting for effect (especially in dialogue or poetic prose)

You don't need to go overboard. Just aim for *clarity with character*. You want your voice to shine through.

Step 6: Ask for Feedback (If You Want It)

This is optional. You *do not* need validation to be proud of your work.

But if you *do* want feedback, be clear about what kind:

- "Can you tell me where it flows well and where it drags?"
- "Does the ending land for you?"
- "What parts confused you, if any?"

Ask someone you trust to be kind and constructive—or submit it to a writing group or contest that offers gentle critiques.

But always come back to *your own voice*. If the feedback helps you make your story stronger *without* losing your spark—great. If it drains your job? You're allowed to ignore it.

Step 7: Define What "Finished" Means to You

Is your goal to:

- Feel proud of what you created?
- Share it on a blog or social page?
- Submit to a contest or lit mag?
- Keep it as a private victory?

You decide what success looks like. A story is finished when *you* say it is.

Final Thought: You Don't Need to "Fix" Everything

Revising isn't about perfection—it's about *intention*. It's about shaping the story, so it feels more like *you*.

If your story made you feel something, if it captured a moment that matters to you, if it gave you joy or catharsis or even a good laugh—that's enough.

Remember: not every story needs to be brilliant. But every story you finish and reflect on will make you a *better*, more joyful writer.

So, revise with care. Polish with pride. And when it's ready—let it fly, or let it rest.

You've made something beautiful. And that's worth celebrating.

CHAPTER TWENTY-SEVEN
Technology Is Your Friend

How to Use Tools to Support Your Writing—Not Replace It

Let's be real: writing can feel a little old-school sometimes. Pen and paper. Solitude. Typewriters if you're feeling vintage. But guess what? We're living in the 21st century, and technology is *totally on your side*.

Whether you're stuck, tired, or just juggling a busy life, there are tools out there that can make writing **easier, smoother, and more fun**—without taking the soul out of your words.

So don't be afraid to lean into a little tech magic. Here are *friendly, non-scary* ways to use technology as your creative sidekick.

1. Talk to Your Phone—Yes, Really

The best ideas come when you're not sitting at a desk. Maybe you're on a walk. In the kitchen. Half-asleep on the couch. That's where *dictation* comes in.

Most smartphones have a built-in **voice-to-text feature**. You talk—it types. It won't always be perfect (you might get the odd "ducking" instead of... well, you know), but it's surprisingly good. And it means you can capture that idea *before it disappears forever*.

Try this:

- Open the Notes app (or Google Docs, or Word)

- Tap the microphone icon on your keyboard.

- Start talking—like you're telling a friend your idea.

Bonus: This is *great* for when you're blocked. Just talk your way into the story. You'll be amazed what comes out.

2. Listen to Your Words Out Loud

Sometimes the best way to *hear* what's working (and what's clunky) is to—well—actually hear it.

Most writing tools now come with **Read Aloud** features, where your computer or phone will literally read your story back to you in a calm, robotic voice (weirdly soothing, honestly).

Here's how:

- In **Microsoft Word**: Go to *Review > Read Aloud*

- In **Scrivener**: Use the built-in *Speech* feature under *Edit > Speech > Start Speaking*

- Or use free tools like **Natural Readers** or **Voice Dream Reader** on your phone.

It helps with:

- Catching awkward phrasing

- Spotting missing words or run-ons

- Hearing your rhythm and flow (super important in short fiction!)

You'll be shocked by what your ears catch that your eyes missed.

3. ChatGPT: Your Pocket-Sized Writing Assistant

Okay, let's talk about AI tools like ChatGPT. These can be *super helpful* in your writing process—but the key is knowing how to use them *well*. Think of it like having a writing buddy who's always available to brainstorm, polish, or just cheer you on.

Here are three *really useful* ways to use ChatGPT (with sample prompts you can copy and paste!):

a) Spell and Grammar Check

Sometimes you just want a second set of eyes to clean things up—without changing your voice. That's where AI editing shines.

Prompt to use:

"Can you please proofread this short story for spelling, grammar, and punctuation only? Don't change my writing style—just fix the technical stuff."

Paste your story right after that prompt, and boom—clean, confident prose in seconds.

b) Review and Editor

Want a more thoughtful read of your story? Ask for a friendly edit with suggestions—just like you'd want from a writing group buddy.

Prompt to use:

"Please review my short story and give me gentle, constructive feedback. Focus on character, structure, clarity, and pacing. Let me know what's working and what could be improved."

This kind of review can help you see your work from a new angle—and give you direction for your next revision.

c) Pretend You're a Competition Judge

Submitting to contests? Want to give your story that extra sparkle? Ask ChatGPT to act like a judge and give you tips for making your story more competitive.

Prompt to use:

"Pretend you're a judge for a short story writing competition. Please review my story and tell me what would make it stand out. What would increase my chances of winning?"

You'll get feedback tailored to impact, originality, and emotional resonance—plus a bit of insight into how your story reads on the first impression.

Words of Caution (and Empowerment)

Tech tools are formidable, but they're here to *support* you—not take over your creativity. Your voice, your perspective, your weird and wonderful ideas—those are the magic.

Use tools to:

- Make the process easier.

- Spark ideas

- Clean up your drafts.

- Boost your confidence.

But always trust your gut. You're the storyteller here.

Final Tip: Don't Be Afraid to Experiment

If a tool doesn't work for you, ditch it. If it sparks something exciting—use it often. Make your writing process feel easier, smoother, and more *yours* with whatever tech helps you feel supported.

You don't have to do everything the "traditional" way. You just have to *keep writing*.

So, talk to your phone. Listen to your story. Ask your AI pal for feedback. And above all—*keep creating with joy*.

Chapter Twenty-Eight
Tips and Tricks to Improve Your Happiness Through Writing

Use Words to Feel Better, Connect More Deeply, and Live More Creatively

Writing is more than just getting ideas out of your head and onto a page. It's a practice—a habit—that can quietly and powerfully increase your happiness. Not just in the "this is fun" way (though yes, fun is important!), but in the deeper sense of helping you feel more *grounded*, more *present*, more *connected* to yourself and others.

Whether you're writing to play, to process, to heal, or just to spend just minutes each day doing something creative, the act of putting words on the page can boost your mood, sharpen your self-awareness, and even shift your perspective.

This section is packed with *practical tools* for writing your way into a happier mindset. You'll find mindfulness exercises, ideas for building uplifting writing communities, joyful ways to share your work, and goal-setting techniques that turn writing into something you look forward to—not something that feels like a chore.

Let's dive into the little rituals, practices, and creative strategies that will make writing one of the *happiest habits* in your life.

Chapter Twenty-Nine

Let Your Writing Be a Friend, Not a Test

This isn't about proving anything. You don't have to be published to be a writer. You don't have to write daily to be resolute. You don't have to write beautifully to write meaningfully.

You just have to write.

Write when you're feeling bold.

Write when you're feeling tender.

Write when you're heart-full and write when you're stuck.

Let writing be a friend you return to. A place you go to figure things out. A tool, a toy, a mirror, a map. Sometimes it will make you laugh. Sometimes it will help you cry. Sometimes it will surprise you in the best possible way.

Chapter Thirty
Growth Happens Quietly, Joyfully

With every story you finish—no matter how small—you build trust in yourself.

With every journal entry, blog post, poem, or half-written scene, you grow.

With every act of writing, you're choosing creativity over passivity, reflection over reaction, meaning over distraction.

You're showing yourself that your inner life matters. That your voice is worth hearing. That joy can be created, not just found.

And slowly, almost without realizing it, you become the kind of person who notices more. Reflects more. Feels more.

In short—you become happier.

Chapter Thirty-One

It's All a Story

One moment. One choice. One line of dialogue. That's all you need to start.

A girl standing in the rain, holding a cake box. A letter found in a library book. A boy who wakes up speaking a language he's never learned.

That's a short story waiting to happen.

So, if you've been telling yourself, you don't have time to write, or your ideas are too small, or your writing isn't "important enough"—this is your invitation to let that go.

Short fiction is small on purpose. That's its magic.

Let it be yours.

Chapter Thirty-Two

The Writer's Journey to Happiness

A Joyful Farewell—and a Beginning

So here we are.

You've wandered through the chapters, tried on prompts like costumes, explored techniques, embraced little wins, and maybe even whispered lines of poetry to yourself in the quiet of the morning. You've learned that writing isn't just a skill or a craft—it's a way of noticing. A way of being. A gentle practice that weaves creativity into your everyday life, moment by moment, word by word.

Now comes the best part: you get to keep going.

Because writing happiness isn't a destination. It's a journey. A spiral. A practice. You don't have to master it. You just have to keep showing up.

There will be days where writing flows like water—easy, light, joyful. There will be days where it feels like wading through molasses. But both kinds of days are part of the path. And here's the quiet truth: every time you choose to write, you're choosing yourself. You're choosing presence. Curiosity. Courage. Joy.

That's powerful.

Chapter Thirty-Three
Ten prompts to get you started

Chapter Thirty-Four

Prompt 9. The Apricot Jam Years — Memoir

We never talked about love, only recipes—handwritten, stained, and passed across generations like precious contraband.

Apricot Jam

Chapter Thirty-Five

Prompt 2. The Lieutenant's Letter – World War I

I opened the envelope with shaking hands; the front line smudged in ink, dirt, and something like regret.

The Lieutenant's Letter

Chapter Thirty-Six

Prompt 3. Ashes and Lace – Historical Romance

She wore black lace to the execution, her heart burning brighter than the torches lining the cobbled square.

Black Lace

Chapter Thirty-Seven

Prompt 4. Lipstick on His Collar — Family Drama / Emotional Fiction

The day I washed lipstick from his collar, the suds turned pink—and I didn't ask whose lips they were.

Lipstick on his Collar

Chapter Thirty-Eight

Prompt 5. The Dragon Princess Drinks Tea Alone – Fantasy/Adventure

My tiara melted along with my last teacup. Mother says fire is a gift, to me it's a curse.

Dragon Princess

Chapter Thirty-Nine

Prompt 6. My Love, My Blade — Romantic Action/Adventure

He blocked my sword like a lover's caress—familiar, fearless. We've fought together. Today, we fight each other.

My Love, my Blade

Chapter Forty

Prompt 7. The Day I Left Him – Memoir/Emotional Realism

I packed the kettle but left the ring. No tears. And a sunrise I could finally see.

The Ring

Chapter Forty-One

Prompt 8. A Kitchen Like a Country — Domestic/Lyrical Fiction

My kitchen smells like my mother's voice—cardamom, lemon, smoke. This is how I return home, bite by bite.

Lemon, Cardomon & Smoke

Chapter Forty-Two

Prompt 9. Little Shoes, Big Goodbye — Parenting/Emotional Fiction

His backpack was bigger than his body. He didn't look back. I waved anyway, just in case.

Big Goodbye

Chapter Forty-Three

Prompt 10. Wind in My Hair, Paris Behind Me — Reflective/Fictional Memoir

I will never drive through Paris with the wind in my hair and a lover at my side.

Wind in my Hair

Other Books by Same Author

Printed in Dunstable, United Kingdom

65265193R00088